# 12 CHEFS OF
# CHRISTMAS

CARLTON **FOOD** NETWORK From the hit TV series

First published in 1999 by HarperCollins*Illustrated*,
an imprint of HarperCollins*Publishers*.

Designed and produced by SP Creative Design
*Editor* Heather Thomas
*Layout Designer* Rolando Ugolini

*Food photographs* Frank Weider
*Home Economists* Jane Lawrie, Karen Taylor (Tony Tobin's dishes)
*Stylist* Judy Williams

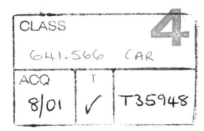
A catalogue record for this book is available from the British Library.

ISBN 0 00 414089 3

Colour origination by Saxon Photolitho
Printed and bound in Great Britain by Scotprint, Musselburgh

CARLTON **FOOD** NETWORK

Whether you live to eat or eat to live, the Carlton Food Network has something to tempt your tastebuds. Europe's only dedicated food channel brings the expertise of the world's finest chefs, food experts and celebrities to television screens around the country.

Carlton Food Network provides an exciting range of programmes featuring celebrity chefs and personalities such as The Nosh Brothers, Brian Turner, Antony Worrall Thompson, Paul Gayler, Ross Burden, Nanette Newman and many more.

There is something on offer for all food lovers: the great programme line-up features a host of shows presented by the country's top chefs, as well as food from every corner of the world - Africa, India, Italy, China, Scotland, England and Ireland, to mention but a few!

The Carlton Food Network has dedicated itself to ensuring that you know all there is to know about healthy eating and nutrition - so you can really enjoy what you eat. Kids can also try out their culinary skills as the Carlton Food Network features some tasty recipes in a great children's programme - and you can find out how to grow the freshest ingredients to use in the kitchen with the Carlton Food Network's very own gardening slot!

In short, the Carlton Food Network has an exciting mix of ingredients which will appeal to all tastebuds!

Tune into Carlton Food Network, TV's tastiest channel for recipes to make your mouth water.

Alex Floyd  Bruno Loubet  Thane Prince  The Nosh Brothers  Tony Tobin  Antony Worrall Thompson  Ross Burden  Mridula Baljekar  Aldo Zilli  Henry Harris  Peter Gottgens  Tessa Bramley

# CONTENTS

MRIDULA BALJEKAR

**MRIDULA BALJEKAR'S** passion for Indian cookery began at an early age in the foothills of the Himalayas where she grew up. She learned the secrets of cooking with spices as she helped to prepare dishes which had been handed down in her family for generations. She later moved to England and has presented 'The Spice Trail' and two series of 'Mridula's Indian Kitchen' for Carlton Food Network. Mridula has written several best-selling books on Indian cookery, is a contributor to many magazines and has developed creative recipes for Indian ready-made meals for a major UK supermarket chain. She is also a demonstrator at the Tante Marie School of Cookery.

**MRIDULA BALJEKAR**

# MENU

## Mridula Baljekar

**serves 6**

# GRILLED SALMON STEAKS

Get your taste buds going by cooking these deliciously spiced salmon steaks for the first course of your Indian-style Christmas Day family meal.

oil, for brushing
6 salmon steaks
juice of 1/2 lemon
2 teaspoons ginger paste
2 teaspoons garlic paste
1/2 teaspoon salt
1 teaspoon coriander seeds
1 teaspoon cumin seeds
2 tablespoons melted butter
1 tablespoon finely chopped fresh coriander

**To garnish:**
crisp lettuce leaves, fresh coriander, chopped cucumber and tomatoes, spring onions and lemon wedges

Line a grill pan with some foil and brush generously with oil. Place the salmon steaks on the prepared foil.

Mix the lemon juice, ginger and garlic pastes and salt together. Gently rub this spice mixture into the fish, turning them in the mixture. Set aside to rest in a cool place for 30 minutes.

Preheat the grill to high and position the grill pan containing the salmon steaks approximately 12.5 cm/5 in away from the heat source. Cook for about 3–4 minutes on one side.

Meanwhile, crush the coriander and cumin seeds with a pestle and mortar. Mix with the melted butter and chopped fresh coriander.

Turn the salmon over and spread the butter evenly over each one. Grill for a further 2–3 minutes. Serve on a bed of lettuce garnished with coriander, cucumber, tomatoes, spring onions and lemon wedges.

# GREEN BEANS IN SPICED BUTTER

Tender green beans, tossed in spiced butter and then cooked in their own juice, are a perfect partner for the marinated spiced turkey.

40 g/1 1/2 oz unsalted butter
1 teaspoon cumin seeds
4 garlic cloves, crushed
1/2 teaspoon freshly milled black pepper
675 g/1 1/2 lb trimmed thin green beans, fresh (blanched) or frozen
1/2 teaspoon salt or to taste

Melt the butter gently in a heavy-based saucepan and add the cumin seeds. Let them sizzle for 35–40 seconds. Add the garlic and stir-fry for a few seconds until it is lightly browned.

Add the black pepper followed by the beans and salt. Cook for 6 minutes over a gentle heat, stirring frequently.

Cover the pan, reduce the heat and let the beans cook in their own juice for 10–12 minutes, until tender, stirring occasionally.

# MARINATED SPICED TURKEY

A complete break from the traditional way of preparing and roasting, this Christmas turkey, with its subtle spicing, is sure to be a hit with all Indian food lovers. Try and choose a small bird because it will absorb the flavours of the spicy marinade right down to the bones. If necessary, cooking two small birds will produce a better result than a single large one. Unlike the traditional roasting method, you need to remove the skin from the turkey before marinating it. It is quicker and easier to use a cloth when pulling the skin back – this will help to prevent it slipping.

1 small turkey, about 3.5 kg/
7 1/2 lb, skin removed

juice of 1 lemon

1 1/2 teaspoons salt

75 g/3 oz whole-milk natural yogurt

1 1/2 tablespoons garlic paste

1 1/2 teaspoons ginger paste

2 teaspoons garam masala

1 teaspoons ground turmeric

1 teaspoon chilli powder or to taste

50 ml/2 fl oz sunflower oil

150 ml/1/4 pint dry white wine

50 g/2 oz butter, melted

**For the stuffing:**

450 g/1 lb minced chicken

1 teaspoon salt

1 teaspoon garlic paste

1 teaspoon ginger paste

1 teaspoon garam masala

1/2 teaspoon freshly milled black pepper

2 tablespoons chopped fresh coriander leaves

1 tablespoon chopped fresh mint leaves or 1 teaspoon dried mint

*(Continued opposite)*

Lay the skinned turkey on its back and make 3 deep incisions right across each breast, and on the outer and inner legs and thighs and the wings. Rub the lemon juice and salt all over the turkey and set aside in a cool place for 30 minutes.

Mix together the yogurt, garlic and ginger paste, garam masala, turmeric and chilli powder. Pour over the turkey, rubbing it well into the incisions. Turn the turkey over and rub the marinade over the back. Transfer to a large dish, cover and refrigerate for 36–48 hours. Remove on Christmas Eve just before going to bed and leave the turkey at room temperature overnight.

Just before you put the turkey in the oven, mix all the ingredients for the stuffing together and use to fill the stomach cavity. Truss the bird securely with some string and place it in a deep roasting pan, breast side down. Pour 200 ml/7 fl oz hot water into the pan around, but not over, the bird and cover loosely with foil – the foil should not touch the turkey.

Cook the bird just below the centre of a preheated oven at 200°C, 400°F, Gas Mark 6 for 45 minutes. Reduce the temperature to 180°C, 350°F, Gas Mark 4 and cook for a further 45 minutes.

Remove the foil and turn the turkey over on its back. Pour the wine all over it, especially the breast meat and legs. Cook for 10 minutes, then baste generously with the melted butter. Cook for a further 30 minutes, basting every 10 minutes with the pan juices. Remove from the oven and allow to rest for 10–15 minutes.

Transfer to a serving plate and strain off all the pan juices into a measuring jug. You should have approximately 425 ml/15 fl oz of cooking juice. If not, make it up to this amount with cold water.

To make the gravy, mix the besan with a little water to a paste and blend it into the turkey stock. Cook over a medium heat, beating all the time with a wire whisk to prevent any lumps forming. Add the white wine and chives and cook for a further minute. Season to taste with salt and pepper and remove from the heat. Carve the turkey into thin slices and serve hot with the gravy.

**For the gravy:**

1 tablespoon besan (chick pea flour)

50 ml/2 fl oz dry white wine

1 tablespoon chopped fresh chives

salt and pepper, to taste

# SPICED POTATOES

For this recipe you need some preboiled potatoes. These can be cooked in advance and safely left in the refrigerator for 2–3 days. The finished dish is quite irresistible, so the amount of potatoes you want to cook is really up to you. The quantity below will give you a generous six portions.

1.5 kg/3½ lb Desirée potatoes

3 tablespoons sunflower or soya oil

50 g/2 oz unsalted butter

1 teaspoon salt or to taste

½ teaspoon garam masala

1 teaspoon ground coriander

1 teaspoon ground cumin

½ teaspoon chilli powder

2 tablespoons chopped fresh mint or 1 teaspoon dried mint

Boil the potatoes in their jackets until tender, then drain and allow to cool completely. Peel the potatoes and cut into 5 cm/2 in pieces.

For a perfect result you will need to fry the potatoes in 2 batches. Heat half of the oil and half of the butter in a large non-stick frying pan over a medium heat. It is important to use a non-stick pan or the potatoes will stick. Add half of the potatoes and increase the heat slightly. Fry the potatoes until they are evenly browned and a light crust forms, stirring and turning them occasionally.

Sprinkle half the garam masala, ground coriander, cumin and chilli powder over the potatoes in the pan. Stir gently until the potatoes are well coated. Stir in half the mint, then remove from the heat and keep warm while you fry the remaining potatoes in the same way.

# PAPAYA AND POMEGRANATE DESSERT

Try and find some good ripe papayas (paw paws) for this recipe. When ripe, the skin has a yellow tinge and feels slightly soft to the touch. If they feel hard, leave them at room temperature for a couple of days. Pomegranates are sold by good supermarkets and Indian stores. They are excellent for adding an exotic touch.

3 small ripe papayas
2 pomegranates
300 ml/10 fl oz double cream
1–2 tablespoons icing sugar
few drops of rosewater or
2 tablespoons Cointreau
fresh mint leaves, to decorate

Trim both ends of each papaya and cut in half lengthways. Carefully ease away the seeds with a teaspoon and discard them. Scrape the white membrane away from the flesh.

Cut the pomegranates in half lengthways, then remove the seeds with a fork and set aside. If the pomegranates are really fresh and ripe, you can peel the outer skin like an orange. Remove and discard the white membrane and pith.

Whip the cream and icing sugar together until light and fluffy, and then gently stir in the rosewater or Cointreau.

Line 6 individual serving dishes with some of the pomegranate seeds and place a papaya half in the centre. Fill the hollow in each papaya with the Cointreau flavoured cream. Top with the remaining pomegranate seeds and decorate with mint leaves. Chill in the refrigerator for a couple of hours before serving.

TESSA BRAMLEY

**TESSA BRAMLEY,** the chef/patron of the highly acclaimed Old Vicarage restaurant in the village of Ridgeway in Derbyshire, was awarded a Michelin star in 1999. She has presented three series for Carlton Food Network – 'Tessa Bramley's Seasonal Kitchen', 'Tessa Bramley's Country Kitchen' and 'Tessa's Tastebuds'. Tessa has written three cookery books.

TESSA BRAMLEY

# MENU

## Tessa Bramley

### STARTER

Potato and smoked salmon pancakes with a rosemary cream sauce

### MAIN COURSE

Roasted fillet of saddle of wild boar with a mustard crust

Red cabbage and juniper cabbage

Sprouts with crispy bacon

Roasted parsnips

Bread sauce

### DESSERT

Tessa's Christmas plum puddings

# POTATO AND SMOKED SALMON PANCAKES WITH A ROSEMARY CREAM SAUCE

These pretty pancakes make a light and delicious first course. If wished, you can make the potato mixture in advance and then cook the pancakes quickly just before serving the Christmas meal.

675 g/1 ½ lb mashed potatoes

3 level tablespoons self-raising flour

3 large eggs

3 tablespoons milk

150 ml/¼ pint double cream

2 egg whites

salt and freshly ground black pepper

freshly grated nutmeg

olive oil, for greasing

85 g/3 oz sliced smoked salmon

rosemary cream sauce (see method), to serve

snipped chives or salmon caviare, to garnish

Mix the mashed potato with the flour, whole eggs, milk and cream. Beat until smooth and then beat in the extra egg whites, seasoning and nutmeg. Continue beating until really smooth. If wished, pass the potato mixture through a sieve into a clean bowl.

Heat a griddle or skillet until evenly hot. Oil it lightly with a little olive oil. Drop some dessertspoonfuls of the potato mixture onto the griddle. The pancakes should hold their shape straight away.

Cut a little of the smoked salmon into small pieces and place on top of the potato pancakes. After about 1 minute, when the underside is golden, flip over each pancake with a palette knife and cook the other side. Roll up the remaining smoked salmon slices into rosettes.

Serve 4 or 6 pancakes per portion garnished with a smoked salmon rosette and surrounded with some rosemary cream sauce. To make this, heat some cream gently in a pan and infuse with a few sprigs of fresh rosemary. Remove the rosemary before serving. Sprinkle the pancakes with snipped chives or garnish with salmon caviare.

# ROASTED FILLET OF SADDLE OF WILD BOAR WITH A MUSTARD CRUST

I like to serve some traditional bread sauce with a bay leaf with this roasted fillet of wild boar. A crab apple and thyme jelly also makes a good accompaniment.

1 x 2.75 kg/6¼ lb fillet of saddle of wild boar

olive oil

salt and freshly ground black pepper

roughly chopped vegetables, e.g. carrots, leeks, onion

1 bay leaf

### For the mustard crust:

2 tablespoons olive oil

2 tablespoons fresh breadcrumbs

½ jar mild grain mustard

1 level teaspoon minced green chilli paste

1 garlic clove, crushed

1 small dessert apple, peeled, cored, grated and then squeezed dry in a cloth

Trim away all the fat and sinew from the wild boar fillet. Rub with a little olive oil and season with salt and pepper. Sear on both sides in a preheated cast iron pan or griddle.

Make the mustard crust. Heat the olive oil in a frying pan and add the breadcrumbs. Cook until the crumbs have absorbed the oil, separated out and have become crisp and brown. Add the remaining ingredients and mix well together.

Spoon the crust mixture over the top of the wild boar fillet, spreading it thickly and evenly and pressing it in well. If possible, set aside in the refrigerator for a few hours to firm up.

Scatter the chopped vegetables and bay leaf in the base of a roasting pan to form a 'trivet' and sit the wild boar on top. Roast in a preheated oven at 220°C, 425°F, Gas Mark 7 for about 20 minutes, and then remove to a warming oven to rest for a further 20 minutes to settle the juices and tenderize the meat. The boar should be very juicy and just slightly pink. If wished, you can use the juices and vegetables in the pan to make some gravy.

Serve the wild boar on a bed of two cabbages – spiced red cabbage and juniper cabbage. Sprouts cooked in lemon oil with crispy thin bacon and roasted parsnips go well with this, as does bread sauce.

## JUNIPER CABBAGE

Heat a glug of olive oil in a saucepan and quickly fry some finely chopped garlic. Add some crushed chopped juniper berries and shredded green cabbage. Stir-fry until the cabbage wilts and turns bright green. Season with salt and add a pinch of sugar.

24

# TESSA'S CHRISTMAS PLUM PUDDINGS

Made without suet, this recipe is much lighter than a normal Christmas pudding but nonetheless dark and rich in fruit. It is baked rather than steamed. The quantities given will make 10 individual puddings or two 600 ml/1 pint puddings.

225 g/8 oz unsalted butter

225 g/8 oz dark muscovado sugar

45 g/1½ oz black treacle

2 large eggs, beaten

50 g/2 oz self-raising flour, sifted

½ level teaspoon ground mixed spice

½ level teaspoon ground cinnamon

½ level teaspoon ground nutmeg

1 rounded tablespoon cocoa powder

150 g/5 oz fresh brown breadcrumbs

grated zest and juice of ½ lemon

1 tablespoon ground almonds

100 ml/3½ fl oz milk

100 ml/3½ fl oz brown ale

50 ml/2 fl oz brandy

50 ml/2 fl oz dark rum

½ small apple, peeled, cored and grated

200 g/7 oz currants

200 g/7 oz sultanas

200 g/7 oz raisins

45 g/1½ oz dried mixed peel, chopped

50 g/2 oz dates, chopped

50 g/2 oz dried apricots, chopped

50 g/2 oz prunes, chopped

50 g/2 oz walnuts, roughly chopped

brandy cream and raspberry purée, to serve

icing sugar, for dusting

Grease 10 individual pudding tins (e.g. 175 ml/6 fl oz dariole moulds) and put circles of greased baking paper in the bases.

Cream the butter, sugar and black treacle. Add the beaten eggs, sifted self-raising flour and spices, cocoa powder and breadcrumbs. Fold all the ingredients together and then add the lemon zest and juice, ground almonds and milk.

Gradually add the ale, brandy and rum, fresh and dried fruits and nuts. Stir everything together and make a wish. Leave the pudding mixture overnight to develop the flavour and darken the colour.

The following day, fill the prepared pudding tins with the pudding mixture and cover with foil. Stand the tins in a bain marie – a roasting pan which is half-filled with water to come halfway up the sides of the pudding tins.

Bake in a preheated oven at 130°C, 250°F, Gas Mark ½ for approximately 2 hours, until the puddings are firm. Allow to cool and then remove from the tins with a firm shake.

Wrap each pudding in food wrap and store in a cool place until Christmas day.

On the day: unwrap puddings, pop back into tins and cover lightly with foil. Reheat in a pre-heated medium hot oven at 200°C, 400°F, Gas Mark 6 for 20–25 minutes until heated through. Test with a skewer. Alternatively, microwave on full power for 2–4 minutes dependant on your oven. Rest for 2–3 minutes and then serve as below.

Serve the puddings with brandy cream and a swirl of sharp raspberry purée to cut through the richness. Dust lightly with icing sugar and top with a festive sprig of holly.

ROSS BURDEN

**ROSS BURDEN,** as Britain's hottest chef, has gone from strength to strength since he burst on to the cooking scene as a finalist on 'Masterchef'. Stylish and self-taught, he was voted one of the UK's top 50 most eligible bachelors by *Company Magazine*. After working in successful restaurants in both New Zealand and London, Ross started The Contemporary Catering Company and his clients include film stars and the Royal Family. He has made numerous TV appearances, including as the host of Carlton Food Network's 'Ross In Thailand', 'Ross on the Range' and 'Ross' Foreign Assignment'. He prepares a Thai–inspired Christmas menu.

**ROSS BURDEN**

# MENU

## Ross Burden

### STARTER

Pork and lemon grass skewers

### MAIN COURSE

Stir-fried king prawns with asparagus and long beans

Steamed Thai fragrant rice

### DESSERT

Mango tart

30

# PORK AND LEMON GRASS SKEWERS

The essence of Thai cooking is speed. These fragrant minced pork skewers are really easy to prepare and can be cooked in minutes. If wished, to save time on Christmas Day, you could make the mixture the night before, then mould on to the lemon grass stalks and chill them in the refrigerator overnight.

300 g/10 oz minced pork
1 tablespoon garlic paste
1 teaspoon finely chopped coriander root
1 teaspoon fish sauce (*nam pla*)
1 teaspoon finely chopped lime leaf
1/2 teaspoon sugar
8 trimmed lemon grass stalks
oil, for deep-frying

**For the sauce:**
6 tablespoons rice vinegar
4 tablespoons caster sugar
1/2 teaspoon salt
1 garlic clove, very finely chopped
2 large red chillies, deseeded and finely chopped
1 teaspoon finely chopped coriander leaves

First make the sauce. Boil the rice vinegar and sugar together to make a syrup, then, off the heat, add the salt, garlic and chillies. Allow to cool and stir in the chopped coriander.

Mix the minced pork with the garlic paste, coriander root, fish sauce, lime leaf and sugar. Mould around the lemon grass stalks and then deep-fry in hot oil at 190°C, 375°F until golden brown Remove carefully from the oil and drain well on absorbent kitchen paper.

Serve hot, preferably on a banana leaf (these are available from specialist Asian food stores), decorated with an orchid.

# STIR-FRIED KING PRAWNS WITH ASPARAGUS AND LONG BEANS

Peel the prawns, taking care to leave the shell intact on the tails, and remove the black vein running along the back. Cut through each prawn a little with a sharp knife and then press out flat to 'butterfly' it.

Fry the garlic in the oil until golden and add the prawns. Turn well and add the asparagus and beans. Keep turning them in the oil to coat them lightly and then add the oyster sauce, fish sauce and sugar. Continue stir-frying and turning the prawns and beans in the sauce over a high heat until the prawns are uniformly pink.

Remove from the pan and divide between 4 serving plates. Sprinkle with chilli slivers and cashew nuts and serve with moulded steamed Thai fragrant rice.

450 g/1 lb raw king prawns with shells

3 garlic cloves, finely sliced

3 tablespoons vegetable oil

175 g/6 oz asparagus tips, cut in half lengthways

150 g/5 oz long beans or thin green beans, cut in 2.5 cm/1 in pieces

4 tablespoons oyster sauce

2 tablespoons fish sauce (*nam pla*)

1 teaspoon sugar

1 red chilli, halved, deseeded and finely sliced

crushed toasted cashew nuts, to garnish

steamed fragrant Thai rice, to serve

# MANGO TART

In Thailand, fresh fruit is most likely to be served at the end of a meal. However, in Britain we love our puddings so here is a sensational dessert with a Thai flavour to round off your festive Thai feast.

225 g/8 oz ready-made puff pastry (preferably ready-rolled)

4 tablespoons lime curd

2 x 400 g/14 oz cans mango slices, drained

a little apricot jam, warmed and sieved

coconut slices, to decorate

icing sugar, for dusting

real vanilla ice cream, to serve

habanero chillies, to garnish (optional)

Roll out the pastry and trim to a rectangle, 30 x 20 cm/12 x 8 in. Cut a border around the inside of the tart with a knife but take care not to cut all the way through the pastry. Transfer to a baking sheet and then prick the pastry all over with a fork.

Spread the lime curd over the pastry, leaving a 2.5 cm/1 in border all the way round. Arrange the mango slices across the pastry in overlapping rows, leaving a 1 cm/½ in border to the pastry. Slightly cut into the edges of the puff pastry with a knife.

Bake the mango tart in a preheated oven at 200°C, 400°F, Gas Mark 6 for about 30 minutes, until lightly browned and the edge of the tart has risen around the filling.

Remove from the oven and paint the sieved apricot jam lightly over the mango slices to glaze them. Scatter with the coconut slices and dust with icing sugar. Serve warm with a scoop of real vanilla ice cream, decorated with habanero chillies (if using).

ALEX FLOYD

**ALEX FLOYD** is Head Chef at Leith's Soho restaurant and Joint Director of Leith's Restaurants. His creative talent in the kitchen was quickly recognised when he joined Leith's Restaurant in Notting Hill as commis chef at the age of nineteen. Within four years he had risen to become one of the youngest head chefs in London, and in 1994, on the twenty-fifth anniversary of Leith's Restaurant, it was awarded its first Michelin star. Alex's dedication to good food and his genuine interest in nurturing young talent have inspired his part-time teaching at Leith's School of Food & Wine, where he is the most popular guest chef.

**ALEX FLOYD**

# MENU

## Alex Floyd

STARTER

Arbroath smokie flans with roast Jurn scallops and red pepper oil

MAIN COURSE

Braised pheasant with whisky and juniper haggis stuffing

DESSERT

Clootie dumpling

Caledonian cream

# ARBROATH SMOKIE FLANS WITH ROAST JURN SCALLOPS AND RED PEPPER OIL

300 g/10 oz Arbroath smokie fillet

3 eggs

200 ml/7 fl oz crème fraîche or mascarpone cheese

juice of 1 lemon

sea salt and freshly ground black pepper

butter, for greasing

6 large scallops

5 tablespoons olive oil

dressed salad leaves and chives, to garnish

**For the red pepper oil:**

3 large red peppers

100 ml/3½ fl oz extra virgin olive oil

1 sprig of rosemary

2 garlic cloves, crushed

1 teaspoon sea salt

salt and ground black pepper

1 tablespoon balsamic vinegar

Prepare the red pepper oil. Place the peppers in a small frying pan or ovenproof dish and add 2 tablespoons of olive oil, the sprig of rosemary, garlic, sea salt and a little ground black pepper. Cook in a preheated oven at 180°C, 350°F, Gas Mark 4 for 20 minutes, turning the peppers occasionally.

Remove from the oven and place the peppers in a bowl. Cover with cling film and set aside. When cool, skin and deseed the peppers, and then force the pepper flesh through a wire sieve into a bowl. Add the vinegar and whisk in the remaining olive oil. Season to taste with salt and pepper and set aside. Alternatively, blend in a blender.

Warm the Arbroath smokie fillet in a preheated oven at 150°C, 300°F, Gas Mark 2 for 5 minutes. This makes it easier to remove the skin and split the fish in two. Remove all the bones and put the flesh in a food processor with the crème fraîche or mascarpone, eggs, lemon juice and seasoning. Purée until smooth.

Spoon the fish mixture into 6 well-buttered small ramekins and stand them in a small roasting pan. Pour some boiling water around the ramekins to come halfway up their sides, then cover with greaseproof paper and cook in a preheated oven at 150°C, 300°F, Gas Mark 2 for about 20 minutes, or until firm and set. Remove and keep warm.

Slice each scallop into 3 equal discs. Season with a little salt and sprinkle with the remaining lemon juice. Add the olive oil to a very hot non-stick frying pan and add the scallops. Roast quickly for 1 minute, until they caramelize and are golden on both sides.

Run a sharp knife around the edges of the ramekins and turn out the flans. Place one in the centre of each serving plate. Drizzle a little of the red pepper oil around the edge of the plate and arrange the scallops round the flan. Top each flan with a little pile of dressed salad leaves and some chives.

# BRAISED PHEASANT WITH WHISKY AND JUNIPER HAGGIS STUFFING

3 x 675 –900 g/1 1/2–2 lb young pheasants

salt and freshly ground pepper

2 tablespoons oil

2 medium onions, finely chopped

2 carrots, chopped

2 celery sticks, chopped

2 garlic cloves, crushed

1 small leek, chopped

300 ml/1/2 pint whisky

300 ml/1/2 pint freshly made chicken stock or made with stock cube

1 tablespoon juniper berries, dry-roasted and crushed

300 ml/1/2 pint whipping cream

1 teaspoon lemon juice

rosemary and bay leaves, to garnish

**For the stuffing:**

1 x 450 g/1 lb haggis

2 tablespoons whisky

1 tablespoon chopped parsley

175 g/6 oz fresh white breadcrumbs

1 whole egg, beaten

salt and pepper

Prepare the stuffing. Place the haggis in a deep saucepan, cover with water and bring to the boil. Reduce the heat and simmer for 8 minutes, then remove and drain. Cut open the haggis and place in a bowl. Add the remaining stuffing ingredients and season to taste. Use this mixture to stuff the pheasants and then secure with string, if wished. Season well with salt and pepper.

Heat the oil in a roasting pan. Add the pheasants and brown them all over. Remove from the pan and set aside. Add the onions, carrots, celery, garlic and leek and lightly brown. Pour half of the whisky over them, set alight and when the flames die down, add the stock and juniper berries. Return the pheasants to the pan.

Cover with foil and bake in the oven at 190°C, 375°F, Gas Mark 5 for about 45 minutes, or until tender — this could take a little longer depending on the age of the birds. Remove the birds, cover with foil and leave to rest while making the sauce.

Strain the pan juices and return them to the roasting pan. Add the remaining whisky, the cream and lemon juice and cook until reduced to a good consistency. Season to taste.

When ready to serve, cut each pheasant into 4 joints, removing the legs and taking the breasts off the bone, and arrange on a serving dish with the stuffing. Spoon the sauce over the top and garnish with rosemary and bay leaves.

# CLOOTIE DUMPLING

This delicious pudding is prepared in the traditional way in an old-fashioned pudding cloth. However, you can use a 1.8 litre/3 pint pudding bowl, covered with some greaseproof paper and secured with string.

1 tablespoon golden syrup

2 tablespoons buttermilk

2 eggs

115 g/4 oz suet, finely chopped

225 g/8 oz self-raising flour

1 teaspoon baking powder

115 g/4 oz fresh breadcrumbs

75 g/3 oz demerara sugar

225 g/8 oz mixed sultanas and currants

1 teaspoon ground cinnamon

1 teaspoon ground ginger

a splash of whisky

icing sugar, for dusting

mint leaves, to decorate

First, prepare the cloth. Half-fill a very large pot with water and bring to the boil. Add a large piece of white cloth or linen cloth to the water and boil for 1–2 minutes. Lift the cloth out with some tongs, allowing any excess water to drip away, and then spread the cloth out flat on a table. Dust a layer of flour over the cloth (this forms the film) and leave flat.

Make the dumpling. Dissolve the syrup in the buttermilk. Add the eggs and beat well with the other ingredients. Place the mixture in the centre of the prepared cloth. Pull up the edges and tie loosely with some string, leaving a little space for the dumpling to expand.

Place an upturned plate in the bottom of a saucepan and then add the dumpling. Pour in water to come two-thirds of the way up the dumpling. Bring to simmering point, cover with a lid and cook for 3 1/2–4 hours, checking the water level occasionally and topping up with boiling water, as necessary.

When you are ready to turn out the dumpling, fill a basin large enough to hold the dumpling with cold water and have ready another bowl into which the dumpling will just fit. First, dip the dumpling into the cold water for about 10 seconds — this prevents the skin sticking to the edge. Now put the dumpling into the empty bowl and untie the string. Open out the cloth and hang it over the sides of the bowl. Put a warm serving plate over the bowl, invert the bowl and turn out the dumpling onto the plate, carefully removing the cloth.

Dust with icing sugar and serve sliced with a spoonful of caledonian cream (see opposite). Decorate with sprigs of fresh mint.

# CALEDONIAN CREAM

50 g/2 oz mascarpone cream cheese

115 ml/4 fl oz double cream

1 tablespoon thick bitter seville marmalade

2 tablespoons brandy (or rum)

2 teaspoons lemon juice

sugar, to taste

Beat the mascarpone cream cheese to soften it a little. Lightly whip the double cream and then fold the mascarpone through the cream along with the marmalade, brandy (or rum) and lemon juice, adding sugar to taste. Serve with the clootie dumpling (opposite).

PETER GOTTGENS

**PETER GOTTGENS** worked for many years in the hospitality industry in South Africa, Italy and England before opening Springbok Café, the first South African cuisine restaurant in the UK. His cooking, which is a fusion of South Africa's many culinary traditions, has received much critical acclaim and media interest. As well as participating in 'The Twelve Chefs of Christmas', Peter has appeared on many television programmes in the UK and South Africa. Springbok Café has been listed in the 1999 Michelin Guide, a first for South African cuisine, and Peter is now planning to open more restaurants, both in this country and around the world.

PETER GOTTGENS

# MENU

## Peter Gottgens

**serves 4-6**

STARTER

Cape crayfish soup

Cape seed loaf

MAIN COURSE

Kudu fillet with Boerewors stuffing

Morogo and samp risotto

Patty-pans

Gem squash

Sweet potatoes

DESSERT

Cape brandy pudding

50

# CAPE CRAYFISH SOUP

You can use either crayfish or lobsters, whichever are available, to make this luxurious South African-style soup. Serve it with Cape seed loaf (below).

2 small cooked crayfish or
2 x 450 g/1 lb lobsters
1 onion, finely diced
1 celery stalk, chopped
1 carrot, diced
2 tablespoons olive oil
250 ml/8½ fl oz white wine
250 ml/8½ fl oz water
500 ml/17 fl oz fish stock
1 teaspoon tomato paste
225 ml/8 fl oz double cream
50 ml/2 fl oz South African sherry
salt and pepper, to taste
fresh herbs, to garnish

Split the crayfish or lobsters in half, remove the tail meat, then dice and reserve for later. Wash what remains of the crayfish under cold running water and break into 3 or 4 smaller pieces.

Sweat off the onion, celery and carrot in the olive oil. Add the white wine together with the crayfish pieces and water. Leave to simmer gently, adding the fish stock, a little at a time, and checking the flavour frequently. Strain after about 30 or 40 minutes.

Pour the strained liquid back into the pan and boil to reduce it further. Stir in the diced crayfish meat, tomato paste and cream.

Add the sherry and check the seasoning just before serving. Ladle into bowls and serve, garnished with fresh herbs of your choice.

# CAPE SEED LOAF

1 teaspoon caster sugar
500 ml/17 fl oz lukewarm water
1 heaped tablespoon dried yeast
200 g/7 oz bran
400 g/14 oz wholemeal flour
75 g/3 oz sunflower seeds
75 g/3 oz pumpkin seeds
50 g/2 oz mixed poppy and
sesame seeds
2 teaspoons salt
75 g/3 oz sultanas (optional)

Put the caster sugar into the lukewarm water in a bowl, and whisk in the dried yeast. Put aside for a few minutes.

Mix the bran, wholemeal flour, sunflower, pumpkin, poppy and sesame seeds and salt in a food mixer or food processor, adding the yeast water slowly. Process, then check that the mixture is thoroughly mixed and moist. If using, add the sultanas to the mixture, mixing in evenly, before dividing it between two well-greased 450 g/1 lb loaf tins.

Leave the loaves in a warm place to prove for about 10 minutes and then bake in a preheated oven at 220°C, 425°F, Gas Mark 7 for about 40 minutes, until risen and cooked.

# MOROGO AND SAMP RISOTTO

In this unusual South African recipe for risotto, the morogo is a fragrant mixture of wilted green leaves whereas the samp consists of maize kernels, or popping corn, which have been soaked overnight before cooking. It goes very well with the Kudu fillet on page 53.

**For the morogo:**

1 tablespoon olive oil

1 onion, chopped

1 garlic clove, crushed

115 g/4 oz spinach leaves, washed

115 g/4 oz beetroot leaves, washed

115 g/4 oz rocket, washed

115 g/4 oz pumpkin tendrils (optional)

150 ml/¼ pint water

2 tablespoons butter

salt, to taste

**For the samp:**

1 large onion, finely chopped

2 garlic cloves, crushed

2 tablespoons olive oil

450 g/1 lb samp (see recipe introduction), soaked overnight in cold water and drained

750 ml/1¼ pints water

1–2 teaspoons salt

To make the morogo, heat the olive oil in a pan and sweat the onion and garlic until softened. Add the greens and water and bring to the boil. With the lid on the pan, continue boiling for 2–3 minutes, stirring once or twice. The vegetable leaves should be bright green and tender. Remove from the heat, then drain off the liquid and reserve. When the vegetables are cool, chop them finely and put to one side while you prepare the samp.

To cook the samp, sweat the onion and garlic in the olive oil in a heavy pan for 2 minutes. Add the drained samp, stirring well to ensure that the samp does not stick to the pan. Add the reserved morogo cooking liquid and enough fresh water to cover the samp.

Cook gently, stirring frequently, for about 15 minutes. Add the salt, being careful not to add too much. Continue cooking, adding more water as and when necessary, until the kernels are soft. Add the morogo mixture and cook gently until the mixture binds.

# KUDU FILLET WITH BOEREWORS STUFFING

Kudu fillet comes from the antelope but you can use venison as an equally delicious alternative. Boerewors is a traditional Afrikaans coarsely ground sausage.

Make the stuffing: mince the venison, pork and kidney fat together – the mixture should be coarsely minced rather than fine. Combine all the stuffing ingredients, mixing well, and put aside.

Wash the kudu fillet and split down the middle. Press it out flat and pack with the boerewors stuffing. Fold the meat back over the stuffing to enclose it and tie securely with string. Rub some salt and pepper into the outside of the fillet and brush with a little olive oil.

Place the kudu fillet in a hot roasting pan and seal it quickly on both sides. Reduce the heat and cook, turning frequently, for about 10 minutes each side, until the kudu is cooked through and the boerewors stuffing has firmed up and is cooked. Alternatively, cook in a preheated oven at 230°C/450°F/Gas Mark 8 for 20–25 minutes.

Remove the meat from the pan and keep warm. Add the diced shallots to the roasting juices in the pan and cook on top of the stove for a few minutes, until the shallots are tender. Add the red wine and cook rapidly until thickened and reduced. Check the seasoning. Serve with the sliced kudu fillet.

1 x 675 g/1½ lb kudu fillet (or loin fillet of venison or beef fillet)
salt and freshly ground pepper
olive oil, for brushing

### For the Boerewors stuffing:

200 g/7 oz venison
75 g/3 oz pork
50 g/2 oz lamb's kidney fat
1 teaspoon salt
1 tablespoon crushed roasted coriander seeds
50 ml/2 fl oz red wine
50 ml/2 fl oz malt vinegar
pinch of ground cloves
pinch of thyme
pinch of oregano

### For the sauce:

2 banana (large) shallots, diced
200 ml/7 fl oz red wine (pinotage)

# PATTY-PANS

450 ml/¾ pint water
pinch of salt
16 patty-pan squash
2 teaspoons butter
1 tablespoon South African sherry

Put the water, salt and patty-pans in a small saucepan. Bring to the boil and remove the patty-pans after about 5 minutes when they are *al dente* (just tender but still a little firm). Drain well.

Melt the butter in a pan and lightly sauté the patty-pans, adding the sherry at the last minute. Cook gently to allow the sauce to thicken slightly, then serve with the kudu fillet.

# GEM SQUASH

4 gem squash
500 ml/17 fl oz water
freshly grated nutmeg, to taste
salt, to taste
4 teaspoons butter

Prick the gem squash once or twice with a knife or fork and put them into a saucepan with the water. Bring to the boil and boil for 7 minutes, or until soft. When tender, remove the squash from the water, drain and allow to cool slightly.

Cut each squash in half and scoop out the pips with either a teaspoon or dessertspoon, then discard. Scoop out the flesh and season to taste with nutmeg and salt. Add a little butter and serve.

# SWEET POTATOES

675 g/1½ lb sweet potatoes
500 ml/17 fl oz water
3 teaspoons acacia honey
2 teaspoons olive oil
1 teaspoon *naartjie* (clementine) zest

Peel the sweet potatoes and cut into large dice. Bring the water to the boil in a large pan and add the diced sweet potato. Blanch for 2–3 minutes, then remove and refresh. Drain well.

Place the sweet potato on a baking tray and drizzle the honey, oil and clementine zest over them. Roast in a preheated oven at 220°C, 425°F, Gas Mark 7 for about 5–10 minutes, until golden brown.

# CAPE BRANDY PUDDING

1 level teaspoon bicarbonate of soda

250 g/9 oz dates, stoned and finely chopped

250 ml/9 fl oz boiling water

115 g/4 oz butter

115 g/4 oz granulated sugar

2 medium eggs, beaten

250 g/9 oz chopped walnuts

225 g/8 oz plain flour

1 level teaspoon baking powder

1/2 teaspoon salt

75 ml/3 fl oz brandy

seasonal berries and whipped cream, to decorate

icing sugar, for dusting

**For the brandy sauce:**

25 g/1 oz butter

115 g/4 oz granulated sugar

100 ml/3 1/2 fl oz water

115 g/4 oz apricot jam

1 teaspoon vanilla essence

pinch of salt

75 ml/3 fl oz brandy

Add the bicarbonate of soda to the dates and pour the boiling water over them. Mix well and leave to cool.

Cream the butter and sugar, then beat in the eggs, one at a time, mixing well. Beat in the dates, together with their soaking liquid, and the walnuts, then sift the flour, baking powder and salt over the creamed mixture and fold in gently. Mix in the brandy and then spoon the batter into a large baking dish.

Bake in a preheated oven at 220°C, 425°F, Gas Mark 7 for approximately 40 minutes, until cooked.

To make the sauce, heat the butter, sugar and water until boiling, then whisk in the jam, vanilla essence and salt. Continue cooking until reduced and slightly thickened. Stir in the brandy.

Pour some of the brandy sauce over the cooked pudding as soon as it comes out of the oven and allow to soak in. Cut the pudding into squares or slices and serve with seasonal berries and cream, dusted lightly with icing sugar. Serve the remaining brandy sauce separately.

HENRY HARRIS

**HENRY HARRIS** worked extensively in the hotel industry before joining the Leith's School of Food & Wine in 1983. Having been introduced to Simon Hopkinson, he worked with him as sous chef at Hilaire in London's Old Brompton Road. In 1987, Henry flew to San Francisco where he had the opportunity to work with Alice Waters, one of America's most respected chefs. After joining up again with Simon Hopkinson at Bibendum, Henry was approached in 1992 to join The Harvey Nichols Fifth Floor Restaurant, Café and Bar as Executive Head Chef. He presented the series 'Thoroughly Modern British' for Carlton Food Network and his Christmas menu is traditionally British.

HENRY HARRIS

# MENU

## Henry Harris

serves 2

### STARTER

Wild mushroom and pecorino tarts

### MAIN COURSE

Entrecôte vigneronne

Celeriac and horseradish compôte

### DESSERT

Date and goat's cheese savoury

# WILD MUSHROOM AND PECORINO TARTS

3 tablespoons olive oil

2 handfuls of mixed oriental mushrooms, e.g. oyster and shiitake, chopped

salt and pepper

1 large garlic clove, finely chopped

zest of ¼ lemon

squeeze of lemon juice

2 tablespoons coarsely chopped flat parsley

2 sheets puff pastry, approximately 15 x 15 cm/6 x 6 in

beaten egg, for glazing

75 g/3 oz young Pecorino cheese, thinly sliced

chopped basil or parsley, to garnish

Heat the olive oil in a frying pan, add the mushrooms and seasoning and sauté briskly until cooked and golden brown. Stir in the garlic, lemon zest and juice and parsley. Remove from the heat and set aside to cool a little.

Roll out the sheets of puff pastry to the required dimensions, They should be the thickness of 2 matchsticks. Don't worry about how symmetrical they are – they are meant to be home-made.

Oil a baking sheet and place the 2 sheets of pastry on it. Prick the pastry all over with a fork and brush around the sides but not right up to the edge with beaten egg.

Arrange the mushrooms in a layer in the middle of each sheet. Cook in a preheated oven at 200°C, 400°F, Gas Mark 6 for 10 minutes, or until golden brown and puffed up round the edge.

Remove from the oven, then top with the Pecorino and return the tarts to the oven for 2–3 minutes. Remove and serve the tarts immediately, sprinkled with chopped basil or parsley.

64

# ENTRECOTE VIGNERONNE

Heat the clarified butter in a heavy frying pan. Season the steaks and fry over a medium heat for approximately 5 minutes on each side until well browned. Remove from the pan, keep warm and let the meat relax. This will help tenderize it.

Tip out the excess fat from the pan, then add the unsalted butter and the shallots and cook gently for 5 minutes. Add the red wine and cook until the sauce has reduced by half.

Add the stock and reduce by half. Check the seasoning, slip in the oysters and their juices and simmer gently for approximately 30–40 seconds. Stir in the chopped parsley.

To serve, place each steak on a large plate, top with the oysters and spoon the sauce over the top. Serve immediately with some celeriac and horseradish compôte (see page 66).

**Note:** To clarify butter, melt some unsalted butter in a saucepan and pour off the clear liquid, discarding the milky solids.

2 tablespoons clarified butter (see note)

salt and pepper

2 x 225 g/8 oz entrecôte steaks

2 tablespoons unsalted butter

2 tablespoons finely chopped shallots

150 ml/¼ pint red wine (preferably Bordeaux)

100 ml/3½ fl oz veal or chicken stock

6 rock oysters, shucked and stored in their juice

1 tablespoon chopped parsley

# CELERIAC AND HORSERADISH COMPOTE

2 tablespoons butter

½ celeriac, peeled and finely shredded

salt and pepper

water or stock

2 tablespoons freshly grated horseradish

Melt the butter in a small saucepan. Add the shredded celeriac. Season with salt and pepper and add a little water or stock. Cover the pan and cook slowly for 15 minutes. Check the seasoning, stir in the horseradish and serve with the entrecôte steaks (see page 64).

# DATE AND GOAT'S CHEESE SAVOURY

Although it is more usual nowadays to serve a sweet dessert at the end of a meal, the traditional alternative used to be a savoury dish, usually accompanied by port.

115 g/4 oz fresh goat's cheese
1/2 garlic clove, mashed
zest of 1/2 lemon
1 small red chilli, deseeded and chopped
salt and pepper
125 ml/41/2 fl oz ruby port
125 ml/41/2 fl oz chicken stock
125 ml/41/2 fl oz balsamic vinegar
1 teaspoon cracked peppercorns
12 Mejdool dates
4 slices brioche
few drops of olive oil (optional)

Combine the goat's cheese, garlic, lemon zest and chilli. Add a pinch of salt and check the seasoning, then set aside.

Mix the port, chicken stock, balsamic vinegar and cracked peppercorns in a saucepan and bring to the boil. Reduce to a light syrup, adding a little more port if wished, and keep warm.

Split each date lengthways, remove the stone and fill with a generous amount of the goat's cheese mixture. Cook under a preheated grill for 6–7 minutes, or until lightly glazed.

Meanwhile, toast the brioche slices and remove the crusts with a pastry cutter. Place a brioche toast on each plate and top with 3 dates. Drizzle the syrup over the top, adding a few drops of olive oil, if wished, and serve immediately.

BRUNO LOUBET

**BRUNO LOUBET** presents 'Chez Bruno' on Carlton Food Network and has written three cookery books. After working in some of the top Parisian restaurants, Bruno came to England where his first job was at Raymond Blanc's Le Manoir Aux Quat' Saisons. In 1985, he was voted the Good Food Guide's Young Chef of the Year. Now the executive chef and consultant to Oliver Peyton's restaurants, Mash, Atlantic and Coast, Bruno previously cooked at the Chelsea Hotel, opened L'Odéon on Regent Street, and gained his first Michelin star at The Four Seasons on Park Lane. His Christmas menu is traditionally French.

# MENU

## Bruno Loubet

serves 6

STARTER

Paupiettes de saumon fumé et crabe, crème d'huitres au curry

MAIN COURSE

Stuffed capon with ceps and chestnuts cooked in a salt crust

DESSERT

Iced lemon and blackcurrant roulade in red wine syrup

# PAUPIETTES DE SAUMON FUME ET CRABE, CREME D'HUITRES AU CURRY

5 tablespoons mayonnaise

250 g/9 oz fresh or frozen crab meat

6 spring onions, chopped

1 tablespoon chopped fresh coriander

1 apple, peeled, cored and diced

1 green chilli, deseeded and chopped

juice of 1/2 lemon

salt and pepper

6 slices smoked salmon

1/2 teaspoon curry paste

3 tablespoons olive oil

6 oysters

1 small bunch of chives, snipped

sprigs of coriander, to garnish

paprika, for dusting

Place 4 spoonfuls of mayonnaise in a bowl with the crab meat, spring onions, coriander, apple, chilli and a little of the lemon juice. Season to taste with salt and pepper, then mix well.

Place each salmon slice on a sheet of cling film and top each of them with a little of the crab mixture. Gently pull the sides of the salmon up around the filling to meet at the top in the centre. Pull the cling film up around the salmon, twisting and squeezing the top of the cling film until you have an enclosed ball of salmon inside. Repeat with the remaining salmon and filling and then chill in the refrigerator.

To make the cream sauce, heat the curry paste in a pan with the olive oil and stir over a low heat for 3 minutes. Put the oysters in a liquidizer with the remaining mayonnaise, the lemon juice and curry oil. Process until smooth.

Place a smoked salmon ball on the middle of each serving plate. Spoon some sauce around it and sprinkle with the chives. Garnish with fresh coriander and dust lightly with paprika.

# STUFFED CAPON WITH CEPS AND CHESTNUTS COOKED IN A SALT CRUST

1 x 3 kg/6½ lb capon
olive oil, for brushing
fresh sage leaves

### For the stuffing:

2–3 tablespoons olive oil
18 shallots, cut in quarters
800 g/1¾ lb ceps or wild mushrooms
115 g/4 oz pancetta, roughly chopped
3 garlic cloves, crushed
200 g/7 oz dried pears, soaked overnight and cut into pieces
2 tablespoons parsley
500 g/1 lb 2 oz chestnuts, boiled in water

### For the salt dough:

200 g/7 oz flour
9 egg whites
750 g/1 lb 10 oz salt

### For the sauce:

500 ml/17 fl oz sauternes or muscat wine
3 tablespoons soy sauce
125 g/4½ oz butter
juice of ¼ lemon
freshly ground black pepper

Make the stuffing. Heat the olive oil in a pan and cook the shallots until coloured, then add the ceps. Toss well and cook until the ceps start to colour, then add the pancetta, garlic, pears and parsley. Peel the chestnuts and add to the stuffing, then set aside to cool.

In a hot pan or roasting pan, colour the capon in a little oil on every side and leave to cool completely. When cool, fill with the stuffing.

To make the crust, place the flour, egg whites and salt in a large bowl and beat with an electric mixer on medium speed for 1 minute. Add just enough water to bind to a dough and then shape into a ball.

Brush the capon with oil and season with pepper. On a lightly floured surface, roll out the salt dough to an oblong, about 8 mm/⅓ in thick. It should be large enough to wrap comfortably around the capon. Scatter the sage leaves in the centre of the salt dough and set the capon on top. Brush the dough on one side of the capon with some beaten egg. Fold one side of the dough over the capon, then lift the other side over to totally enclose the capon in the dough. Seal the joints thoroughly with the beaten egg, pressing down firmly with your fingers.

Place the capon, seam down, on a baking sheet and bake in a preheated oven at 150°C, 300°F, Gas Mark 2 for 1 hour 45 minutes. Remove from the oven and set aside to rest for 30 minutes.

To make the sauce, put the sauternes or muscat in a pan with the soy sauce and cook until reduced. Whisk in the butter and finish the sauce with a squeeze of lemon and a grinding of pepper.

Take the capon to the table in its crust. Cut around the crust and remove the top, then lift out the capon and discard the sage. Carve the capon and serve with the stuffing and sauce.

# ICED LEMON AND BLACKCURRANT ROULADE IN RED WINE SYRUP

400 g/14 oz frozen blackcurrants
300 g/10 oz sugar
750 ml/1¼ pints red wine
1 bay leaf
½ lemon, sliced
½ orange, sliced
300 g/10 oz mixed red and white grapes in small bunches
sugar syrup, for dipping
caster sugar, for sprinkling
Grand Marnier, for sprinkling
6 tablespoons lemon curd
600 ml/1 pint vanilla ice cream
300 ml/½ pint double cream, whipped stiffly
some fresh mint leaves, to decorate

**For the biscuit:**

4 eggs, separated
88 g/3 oz caster sugar
50 g/2 oz flour
25 g/1 oz ground almonds

Make the biscuit. Using an electric whisk on a medium speed, beat the egg whites to form soft peaks. Gradually add the caster sugar and continue beating until the mixture is shiny and forms firm peaks. At a lower speed, add the egg yolks and beat until well mixed.

With a spatula, gently fold in the flour and the ground almonds. Spread the mixture in a rectangle, 32 x 25 cm/13 x 10 in, over some greaseproof paper. Bake in a preheated oven at 180°C, 350°F, Gas Mark 4 for 8–10 minutes, then remove and leave to cool on a wire cooling tray.

Place the blackcurrants in a pan with 100 g/3½ oz of sugar and cook slowly until the mixture has a jammy consistency. Remove from the heat and set aside to cool thoroughly.

Bring the wine to the boil with the remaining sugar, bay leaf and orange and lemon slices, then simmer until reduced and very syrupy. Pass through a fine sieve and set the syrup aside.

Dip the grapes in some thick sugar syrup and then into some caster sugar and leave to dry for a few hours.

Spread out a damp cloth on a work surface and place the biscuit on top. Sprinkle with Grand Marnier. Spread with half of the lemon curd, top with the blackcurrant 'jam' and vanilla ice cream. Then cover with the remaining lemon curd.

Roll up like a swiss roll and wrap in cling film. Place in the freezer for 4 hours. Remove and cover the roulade with the whipped cream – pipe it, if wished. Replace in the freezer.

Decorate the top of the roulade with some of the frosted grapes. Cut into slices, surround with the remaining frosted grapes and mint leaves, and serve with some of the red wine syrup.

THE NOSH BROTHERS

**MICK AND NICK NOSH** have hosted several popular cookery series on the Carlton Food Network, including 'Winter Nosh', 'Nordic Nosh', 'Red Hot & Smokin' and 'Costa del Nosh'. Before joining forces in 1992, they both enjoyed successful careers in the music, entertainment and media industries, having served their apprenticeship in famous kitchens around the world. Mick and Nick run their own eponymous restaurant in Notting Hill Gate, London. Renowned for their celebrity parties, they have also written four cookery books and have earned a reputation for first-class entertaining and honest 'food with attitude'.

# THE NOSH BROTHERS

# MENU

## The Nosh Brothers

serves 6

### STARTER
Electric soup

### MAIN COURSE
Roast crown of turkey
with truffles on a bed of
pistachio stuffing

### DESSERT
American crust apple pie

# ELECTRIC SOUP

Otherwise known as Bloody Mary Soup, this first course is extremely simple to make. It helps to chill all the vegetables slightly before juicing them.

300 ml/½ pint fresh juiced carrot, celery and mild onion

1 litre/1⅔ pints fresh juiced Italian plum (or vine) tomatoes

½ teaspoon freshly ground black pepper

⅔ teaspoon celery salt

3 shakes of Tabasco, or to taste

7 shakes of Worcestershire sauce

2 tablespoons mild horseradish sauce

juice of ½ lemon

juice of 1 lime

200 ml/7 fl oz good-quality vodka, e.g. Absolut or peppered vodka

8 tomatoes, skinned, deseeded and finely chopped

4 tablespoons chilli sherry (see right)

celery leaves, to garnish

Use a mechanical juice extractor to juice the vegetables and tomatoes. Add salt and pepper to taste, and celery salt, Tabasco, Worcestershire sauce, horseradish, citrus juices and vodka and then stir in the finely chopped tomato pulp. This adds texture to the soup.

Finally, add the chilli sherry, tasting as you add. It can be very hot and you may need less than the measurement given. Serve the soup chilled and garnished with celery leaves.

## CHILLI SHERRY

This culinary secret was shown to Mick by some local Maltese chefs as a way of livening up fish soups. It has become a Nosh tradition for sharpening up Bloody Marys.

Into a sterilized white wine (clear glass) bottle place 4 large whole fresh red chillies, which have been previously blanched for 15 seconds in boiling water. Pour over them a bottle of dry sherry, such as a fino – cream or medium sherries do not seem to work so well. Leave to steep for 3–4 weeks before using. Try adding a few drops to risottos, gravies, soups and sauces.

84

# ROAST CROWN OF TURKEY WITH TRUFFLES ON A BED OF PISTACHIO STUFFING

10 slices white Alba truffles
(or firm mushrooms)

few drops of truffle oil

1 large crown fresh turkey breast,
with bone and skin (use a good
bronze variety)

3 tablespoons melted butter

sea salt and freshly ground
black pepper

watercress and grapes, to garnish

**For the stuffing:**

50 g/2 oz slightly salted butter

1 medium onion, finely chopped

2 rashers smoked bacon, rind
removed and finely chopped

1 large cooking apple, peeled,
cored and chopped

1 garlic clove, crushed

*(Continued opposite)*

Make the stuffing. Heat the butter in a frying pan and gently cook the onion and bacon until soft and golden. Add the apple and garlic and fry for 1 minute, then add the pistachios. Remove the pan from the heat and add the breadcrumbs and grapes, mixing well.

To this mixture add the chicken stock together with the orange juice, wine and chopped herbs. Season with salt and pepper. Drape a very large sheet of foil over a roasting pan and place the mound of stuffing in the middle in a shape that will fit snugly under the turkey.

Marinate the truffles in the truffle oil. If you cannot obtain them or, indeed, afford them, use mushrooms instead.

Place the turkey on top of the stuffing in the roasting pan. Make small slits in the skin of the bird and slide the small infused slivers of truffle or mushroom under the skin. If wished,

you can inject the remaining truffle oil under the skin, using a syringe. Brush the turkey with melted butter and season with salt and pepper.

Pull the foil up around the turkey to enclose it and keep it moist. Roast in a preheated oven at 200°C, 400°F, Gas Mark 6 for about 1¼ hours. Reduce the temperature slightly for fan ovens.

Then increase the oven temperature to 220°C, 425°F, Gas Mark 7 for another 15 minutes, having removed the foil to brown the top of the turkey and crisp it up.

To allow easy carving, rest the turkey crown for 10 minutes under the foil before carving it. Any juice that runs out of the meat while it is 'resting' should be absorbed by the stuffing mixture.

Serve, garnished with watercress and grapes, with an American-style dish of fettuccine with wild mushrooms and some creamed spinach with bacon and onion.

150 g/5 oz shelled pistachios, roughly chopped

2 slices white bread, crusts removed and finely crumbed

50 g/2 oz red or black seedless grapes, halved

2–3 tablespoons chicken stock

juice of ½ orange

115 ml/4 fl oz white wine

1 tablespoon chopped fresh thyme

1 tablespoon chopped fresh parsley

salt and freshly ground black pepper

# AMERICAN CRUST APPLE PIE

This is a traditional apple pie — just like Momma used to make!

225 g/8 oz plain flour

1/2 teaspoon salt

6 tablespoons chilled unsalted butter

115 g/4 oz vegetable shortening,
e.g. Trex

1 tablespoon caster sugar

6–8 tablespoons iced water

6 drops of vanilla extract

caster sugar, for sprinkling

cream or vanilla ice cream, to serve

**For the filling:**

1.1 kg/2 1/2 lb firm tart apples,
e.g. Bramley, peeled, cored and cut
into 3 mm/1/8 in slices

3 1/2 tablespoons plain flour

50 g/2 oz granulated white sugar

50 g/2 oz soft dark brown
muscovado sugar

1/4 teaspoon ground nutmeg or
mace

1/2 teaspoon ground cinnamon

pinch of ground cloves

4 teaspoons melted unsalted butter

1 tablespoon lemon juice

grated zest of 1/2 orange

**For the glaze:**

2 tablespoons milk

2 tablespoons caster sugar

Make the pastry. Sift the flour and salt into a large mixing bowl and cut up the butter and shortening with 2 cold stainless steel knives until the butter and flour combine and the pieces are in small fragments. The mixture should range from breadcrumbs to dried-pea-sized lumps. Sprinkle the sugar over the top.

Sprinkle some iced water, 1 tablespoon at a time, over the mixture with the vanilla extract and mix in gradually with a large tined fork, adding more iced water as necessary, until all the dough is gathered together into one whole ball.

Roll the pastry dough out into a circle, about 15 cm/6 in in diameter, and cover with cling film. Leave to rest in the refrigerator for at least 2 hours. Divide the dough into 2 pieces, one of which is larger than the other. Roll out the larger piece of dough on a floured surface into a 32 cm/13 in circle. The pastry should be about 3 mm/1/8 in thick. Roll the pastry onto the rolling pin and drape it loosely into a greased and floured 22 cm/9 in pie dish.

Push the dough, taking care not to stretch it, into the corners of the dish and trim the pastry into a disc with 2.5 cm/1 in overhang. Fold the 'excess' under the rim of the pan and flute the top with the back of a knife. Roll out the remaining dough for the lid.

Prick the base of the pie with a fork, then line with foil and place some dried baking beans on the base to hold its shape while baking 'blind'. Bake in a preheated oven at 230°C, 450°F, Gas Mark 8 for 10 minutes, then reduce the oven temperature to 200°C, 400°F,

Gas Mark 6. Remove the beans and foil and bake the pie crust for a further 3–4 minutes. Ensure that the pastry does not become over-brown. Set aside to cool.

Make the filling. In a bowl, mix the apple, flour, sugars and spices, tossing them together evenly. Sprinkle with the melted butter, lemon juice and orange zest and combine thoroughly.

Spoon the apple mixture into the pie dish, piling it slightly high in the centre, and place the rolled out pastry cover over the top. Wet the edges with water and press the cover onto the base pastry. Make a slit in the centre for the steam to escape, then brush the pie with milk and sprinkle with sugar.

Bake on the middle shelf in a preheated oven at 230°C, 450°F, Gas Mark 8 for 10 minutes, then reduce the temperature to 180°C, 350°F, Gas Mark 4 for another 30–40 minutes, until the top of the pie is golden or, at least, until the bottom crust is golden. Serve with lashings of cream or real vanilla ice cream.

THANE PRINCE

**THANE PRINCE** has presented four cookery series on the Carlton Food Network, – 'Japaneasy', 'Retrospectives' with Antony Worrall Thompson, 'Taste of England' and 'Food from the Village'. Thane has written seven books, writes about food and cooking in the *Weekend Telegraph* and contributes to numerous magazines. She is the co-proprietor of the Aldeburgh Cookery School in Suffolk as well as regularly teaching at Alastair Little's schools in Italy and giving cookery demonstrations and talks about the enjoyment of good food.

THANE PRINCE

MENU

# Thane Prince

serves 6

## STARTER

Grilled king prawns with Thai dipping sauce

## MAIN COURSE

Butterfly leg of lamb

Mint jelly

Roasted pumpkin

Garlic potato packets

## DESSERT

Pavlova

92

# GRILLED KING PRAWNS WITH THAI DIPPING SAUCE

This is the delicious first course for a genuine Aussie barbecue. In Australia, we enjoy Christmas in the hot sun in the garden or on the beach. Don't be disheartened by the British weather – get out into the garden and start barbecueing!

18 large raw king prawns
a little seasoned oil
sliced lime and fresh coriander, to garnish

**For the Thai dipping sauce:**
115 g/4 oz block coconut cream
50 ml/2 fl oz warm water
grated zest and juice of 3 limes
2 teaspoons caster sugar
1 tablespoon fish sauce
2 tablespoons light soy sauce
1 large red chilli, deseeded and chopped

Carefully shell and devein the king prawns, leaving on the tail section. Cut down through the back of each prawn, but not right through, and open out like a butterfly.

Brush the prawns lightly with seasoned oil and cook on a preheated barbecue or a ridged griddle pan for 3 minutes each side. As they cook, they will turn pink and opaque.

Place all the ingredients for the dipping sauce in a blender or food processor and process until well blended, smooth and finely chopped. Serve with the hot grilled king prawns and garnish with slices of lime and fresh coriander.

# GARLIC POTATO PACKETS

Serve these delicious potatoes in individual foil parcels with the lamb on the following page. Cook the potatoes in advance and then barbecue them just before serving.

8 large new potatoes, approximately 675 g/1 1/2 lb
85 g/3 oz butter, softened
2 large garlic cloves, crushed
bunch of fresh parsley or coriander, finely chopped
a good squeeze of lemon juice
Tabasco, to taste
salt and freshly ground black pepper

Scrape the new potatoes and boil them in plenty of salted water until the tip of a knife meets a little resistance when inserted into the centre of a potato. Drain thoroughly and, when cool enough to handle, slice the potatoes into 5 mm/1/4 in slices.

Blend the softened butter with the garlic and chopped herbs, adding some lemon juice, Tabasco and seasoning to taste.

Cut out 6 sheets of foil, about 30 cm/12 in square, and spoon a little pile of potato slices onto each square. Top each potato portion with a spoonful of the garlic butter.

Gather the corners of the foil together to enclose the potatoes and seal well. Keeping the gathered end uppermost, cook the foil parcels on a barbecue over hot coals for 10 minutes, until the potatoes are cooked and tender, and the garlic butter has melted.

# ROASTED PUMPKIN

While you are grilling the butterfly lamb (see page 94), make room on the barbecue for these tender orange slices of pumpkin. Serve with the cooked lamb.

1 small pumpkin or 2 butternut squash
115 ml/4 fl oz olive oil
salt and freshly ground black pepper
fresh thyme leaves
1 garlic clove, crushed

Cut the pumpkin or butternut squash into wedges, scraping out all the seeds and removing the thick outer peel.

Brush with seasoned oil, scatter with thyme and garlic and grill on the barbecue until charred on the outside but cooked through, turning occasionally. The pumpkin will take about 30 minutes to cook.

94

# BUTTERFLY LEG OF LAMB

You can ask your butcher to open out the leg of lamb and remove the bone, in which case your preparation time will drop to five minutes. Alternatively, take a sharp knife and cut down through the meat until you reach the bone, carefully easing the meat away on either side but keeping it in one piece.

Remove the bone, cut off some of the sinew and lay the meat on a board. Make several deep slashes into, but not through, the flesh to open out the thickest parts. Turn over and make some more deep incisions into the skin side.

Season the lamb well with salt and ground black pepper, drizzle with olive oil and scatter the thyme leaves over the joint. Leave to marinate in a cool place until needed.

When you are ready to cook the lamb, place it, skin side down, on a hot barbecue grill and cook for about 10 minutes to seal it before turning and cooking the other side for 10 minutes.

Continue to turn and cook the meat, basting with a little extra oil, until the lamb is cooked to your liking – about 1 hour for rare, 1¼ hours for pink, and 1½ hours for well done.

Remove the meat from the barbecue and let it rest on a carving board for 10 minutes before carving into slices. Serve the lamb with mint jelly.

1 x 1.8 kg/4 lb leg of lamb
salt and freshly ground black pepper
olive oil
fresh thyme leaves
mint jelly, to serve

# PAVLOVA

This quintessential Aussie dessert can be dressed up for Christmas with a selection of colourful fresh fruit and some gold and silver coated chocolate money.

3 large egg whites
3 tablespoons cold water
225 g/8 oz caster sugar
1 teaspoon vinegar
1 teaspoon vanilla essence
3 teaspoons cornflour

**For the topping:**
600 ml/1 pint double cream
juice and grated zest of 1 orange
2–3 tablespoons orange brandy
fresh fruit, e.g. passion fruit, pomegranate seeds, raspberries, blueberries, blackberries, redcurrants or strawberries
gold and silver coated chocolate coins

Beat the egg whites in a clean, dry bowl with a clean whisk until stiff. Add the cold water and continue beating. Gradually add the caster sugar, beating all the time, and then whisk in the vinegar, vanilla essence and cornflour.

Spoon the meringue onto a piece of greaseproof paper on a greased baking sheet. Form the meringue into a 20 cm/8 in circle, wiping the pallet knife around the edge to straighten the sides and top. It is very important to pile the meringue high and not to spread it out.

Cook the Pavlova in a preheated oven at 150°C, 300°F, Gas Mark 2 for 45 minutes. Turn off the oven and then leave the Pavlova to cool inside the oven. Carefully remove the greaseproof paper from the base and transfer to a serving plate.

Make the topping. Whip the cream until it begins to stiffen. Add the orange juice and zest and orange brandy, and continue whisking until quite stiff. Pile the cream on to the cool Pavlova, then decorate with fresh fruit and gold and silver coated chocolate coins.

TONY TOBIN

**TONY TOBIN** has presented his own vegetarian series, The 'Green Gourmet', for Carlton Food Network as well as appearing in '12 Chefs of Christmas'. After working under Brian Turner at the Capital Hotel, and then for Nico Ladenis at Simply Nico and Chez Nico, Tony became Head Chef at the South Lodge Hotel in Lower Bedding. During his time there, the restaurant was awarded the Good Food Guide's Country Restaurant of the Year. Tony is now Executive Chef at the Dining Room and The Bistro in Reigate and a director of Tortellini's Italian restaurants chain. His love of vegetarian food inspired this vegetarian Christmas menu.

TONY TOBIN

# MENU

## Tony Tobin

**serves 6**

### STARTER

Orange scented broth of winter vegetables

### MAIN COURSE

Spicy festive strudel with apricots and Stilton

Brussels sprouts

Green beans

Roast or mashed potatoes

### DESSERT

Caramelized rice pudding with a compôte of winter fruits

# ORANGE SCENTED BROTH OF WINTER VEGETABLES

This colourful soup makes a light and refreshing start to your festive meal. The beauty of it is that you can make it in advance on Christmas Eve and then all you need to do is simply reheat it on Christmas Day.

1 onion, finely chopped

2–3 tablespoons olive oil

2 turnips, diced

2 carrots, diced

1 fennel bulb, diced

2 leeks, diced

2 celery hearts, diced

175 g/6 oz fine green beans, chopped

8 new potatoes, diced

salt

4 tomatoes, skinned, deseeded and chopped

450 g/1 lb baby spinach, trimmed and washed

garlic mayonnaise and crusty bread, to serve

**For the orange stock:**

grated zest of 1 orange

juice of 2 oranges

1 teaspoon tomato purée

5 tablespoons olive oil

1/2 garlic clove, crushed

900 ml/1 1/2 pints water

1 bay leaf

1 sprig of fresh thyme

Make the orange stock. In a large bowl, whisk together the orange zest and juice, tomato purée, olive oil and garlic. Add the water, bay leaf and thyme and set aside for later.

In a large saucepan, fry the onion gently in the olive oil until it softens and turns golden brown. Add all the diced vegetables and stir over a low heat for a few minutes.

Add the orange stock and bring to the boil. Season to taste with a little salt and then lower the heat and cook gently for about 20 minutes, until the vegetables are tender but still firm.

Add the chopped tomatoes and then the spinach to the broth. Heat through gently until the spinach wilts. Check the seasoning and serve the broth with garlic mayonnaise and crusty bread.

104

# SPICY FESTIVE STRUDEL WITH APRICOT AND STILTON

1 carrot, cut into batons

1 parsnip, cut into batons

1 leek, cut into batons

1 swede, cut into batons

1 turnip, cut into batons

1 sweet potato or yam, cut into batons

15 g/½ oz butter

pinch of ground cumin

pinch of ground cinnamon

pinch of ground allspice

1 onion, finely chopped

grated zest of 1 lemon

pinch of fresh thyme or
1 tablespoon chopped coriander

10 dried apricots, chopped

115 g/4 oz Stilton, crumbled

salt and freshly ground black pepper

1 pack filo pastry

175 g/6 oz melted butter

beaten egg yolk, for brushing

coarse sea salt

Blanch the carrot, parsnip, leek, swede, turnip and sweet potato or yam batons in boiling water until just tender but still slightly firm in the middle. Drain well and set aside.

Heat the butter, add the spices and sweat the onion gently until soft and transparent. Add the lemon zest, thyme or coriander and drained vegetable batons and cook for 2 minutes.

Remove from the heat and set aside to cool. Add the apricots and Stilton, mix well and season to taste with salt and pepper.

Unfold the filo pastry and, using a pastry brush, brush 1 sheet with some of the melted butter. Place another sheet on top and carefully rub smooth with your hands. Repeat with 2 more sheets and then again so that you have 3 x two-layer sheets. Brush the edges of the longer sides with butter and join together to make one big rectangle.

Spread the vegetable mixture down the centre and fold the long sides of the filo pastry over the filling so that they meet at the top. Seal securely and then seal and trim the ends. Put it seam-side down on a greased baking sheet, brush with egg yolk and sprinkle with sea salt. Bake in a preheated oven at 180°C, 350°F, Gas Mark 4 for about 30 minutes, until crisp and golden. Cut diagonally into slices and serve with Brussels sprouts and roast or mashed potatoes.

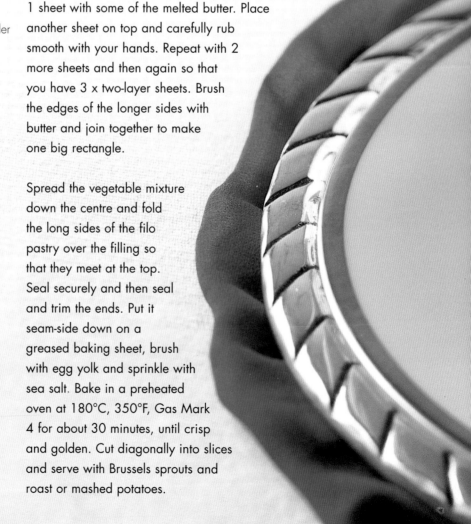

# CARAMELIZED RICE PUDDING WITH A COMPOTE OF WINTER FRUITS

6 prunes, coarsely chopped

6 dried apricots, coarsely chopped

6 pieces dried apple, coarsely chopped

6 pieces dried pear, coarsely chopped

6 dried figs, coarsely chopped

cream, to serve

icing sugar, for dusting

**For the syrup:**

225 g/8 oz sugar

300 ml/1/2 pint water

grated zest and juice of 1 orange

grated zest and juice of 1/2 lemon

1 stick cinnamon

1 bay leaf

2 cloves

1 vanilla pod

Grand Marnier, to taste

**For the rice pudding:**

2 vanilla pods, split

300 ml/1/2 pint double cream

300 ml/1/2 pint milk

grated zest of 1/4 lemon

150 g/5 oz pudding rice

300 g/10 oz sugar

2 eggs, separated

Make the syrup. Put all the ingredients in a saucepan and cook gently for 1 hour, until they form a light syrup. To make the compôte, pour the syrup over the chopped dried fruits and leave to steep until cold.

Scrape the seeds from the vanilla pods. In an ovenproof saucepan, boil the cream, milk, lemon zest and vanilla seeds. Stir in the rice and cover with greaseproof paper.

Bake in a preheated oven at 150°C, 300°F, Gas Mark 2 for about 30 minutes, until tender. Remove the pan from the oven and stir in 100 g/3½ oz of the sugar. Leave to cool.

In a saucepan, dissolve the remaining sugar over a low heat and then boil until it caramelizes. Pour into 6 well-buttered individual metal pudding moulds. Allow to cool.

Remove the greaseproof paper covering from the rice and beat in the egg yolks. Whisk the egg whites in a clean bowl until stiff and fold into the rice. Divide between the caramel-lined moulds and cover with some buttered foil. Bake in the preheated oven for 25 minutes, until they have risen and are firm to the touch.

To serve, unmould the rice puddings onto 6 warm serving plates and spoon a generous amount of fruit compôte around each pudding. Serve with cream, dusted with icing sugar.

# ANTONY WORRALL
# THOMPSON

**ANTONY WORRALL THOMPSON**

**ANTONY WORRALL THOMPSON** worked in several top London restaurants before opening the fashionable Ménage à Trois in Knightsbridge in 1981. As a consultant, he helped launch many successful restaurants, including dell'Ugo, Zoe, Atrium and Palio. In 1997, he set up his own restaurant, Woz, and this was quickly followed by Wiz and Bistrorganic. The winner of numerous culinary awards, Antony has presented six series for Carlton Food Network – 'Antony Worrall Thompson Cooks', Antony's Scotland', 'So You Think You Can't Cook', 'Simply Antony', 'More Simply Antony' and 'Antony's Morocco', as well as writing several best-selling cookery books.

# MENU

## Antony Worrall Thompson

### STARTER

Marinated prawns with tomato and cardamom salsa

### MAIN COURSE

Roast grouse with cotechino stuffing and pangrattato

Green polenta

### DESSERT

Ricotta fruit cake

# MARINATED PRAWNS WITH TOMATO AND CARDAMOM SALSA

Butterfly the prawns by cutting through the back of each one with a pair of scissors, leaving the tail end intact. Cut in slightly with a knife and fold back to devein. Open the prawns and press them out flat.

Arrange the prawns on a tray and sprinkle with the lemon juice, chilli, garlic, and salt and pepper. Drizzle liberally with the olive oil. Cover and leave to marinate for 2–3 hours in the refrigerator.

Meanwhile, make the salsa. Heat the oil until very hot and then add the onion, ginger, garlic and salt. Cook gently for 5 minutes, stirring to prevent the onion and ginger burning. Add the spices and cook for 5 minutes, then add the tomatoes and cook slowly for 20 minutes. Do not allow to dry out, add extra water if required.

Remove the prawns from the marinade and cook on a chargrill or oiled cast iron griddle pan for 2 minutes, shell-side down. Serve with the tomato and cardamom salsa, garnished with coriander and lemon wedges.

1 kg/2 lb 4 oz raw king prawns, shells on and heads removed

juice of 1 lemon

1 large red chilli, deseeded and finely diced

2 garlic cloves, finely diced

salt and freshly ground black pepper

150 ml/¼ pint extra virgin olive oil

fresh coriander and lemon wedges, to garnish

### For the tomato and cardamom salsa:

5 tablespoons olive oil

1 large onion, finely diced

2 large pieces of ginger, peeled and finely diced

10 garlic cloves, finely diced

1 tablespoon sea salt

1 teaspoon ground turmeric

6 cloves, roasted and ground

8 cardamom pods, roasted and ground

10 tomatoes, skinned, deseeded and diced (or use canned tomatoes)

# ROAST GROUSE WITH COTECHINO STUFFING AND PANGRATTATO

6 grouse or partridge

12 slices prosciutto or Parma ham

4 tablespoons olive oil

3 garlic cloves, finely chopped

1 onion, finely chopped

1 teaspoon fresh thyme leaves

115 g/4 oz dried porcini, soaked for ½ hour, drained, squeezed and chopped (soaking liquor reserved)

115 g/4 oz chicken livers, chopped

350 ml/12 fl oz dry red wine

a little butter, to enrich the sauce

salt and freshly ground black pepper

**For the cotechino stuffing:**

2 small red onions, finely chopped

2 garlic cloves, finely chopped

2 celery stalks, finely chopped

1 carrot, finely chopped

½ teaspoon fresh thyme leaves

3 tablespoons good olive oil

1 cotechino sausage, casing removed (Italian spicy sausage)

12 fresh sage leaves, chopped

115 g/4 oz chicken livers, diced

250 ml/8 fl oz dry red wine

75 g/3 oz soft white breadcrumbs

salt and freshly ground black pepper

Make the stuffing. Cook the onion, garlic, celery, carrot and thyme in the oil until soft but not brown. Crumble the cotechino into the onion mix with the sage and fry for 10 minutes. Add the chicken livers and cook for a further 2 minutes. Add the wine and then boil until reduced by half. Season with salt and pepper, allow to cool, and then fold in adequate breadcrumbs to bind the stuffing.

Stuff the birds with the cotechino stuffing, and then wrap each one in 2 slices of prosciutto or Parma ham.

Heat 2 tablespoons of the olive oil in a pan and cook the garlic, onion, thyme, chopped porcini and chicken livers until the onion begins to soften. Add the mushroom soaking liquid and cook gently until all the liquid has evaporated. Set aside.

Preheat the oven to its hottest setting. In a roasting pan, heat the remaining olive oil and brown the birds on each side. Roast in the hot oven for 10 minutes, then remove and turn the birds over. Add the porcini mixture and wine and then roast for a further 5 minutes.

Remove the birds and keep warm. Place the roasting pan on the hob, stir the pan juices and, over a moderate heat, whisk in a little butter to enrich them. Check the seasoning.

Sprinkle the grouse with the pangrattato (see opposite) and serve with the porcini mixture and green polenta (see opposite).

# PANGRATTATO

500 ml/17 fl oz olive oil

10 garlic cloves

1 ciabatta loaf, crumbed

3 tablespoons each chopped thyme and marjoram

Heat the olive oil and add the garlic cloves. Cook gently until the garlic turns a deep golden colour, then remove the garlic from the oil and reserve for another use.

Add the breadcrumbs to the oil and cook until deep golden. At the last moment, add the chopped herbs and remove from the heat. Use to sprinkle over the grouse.

# GREEN POLENTA

What makes this recipe so special is that the polenta is cooked in chicken stock instead of water, which gives it a wonderful flavour.

3 leeks, washed and finely sliced

250 g/9 oz unsalted butter

350 g/12 oz greens, e.g. kale, spinach, rocket, flat-leaf parsley

salt and freshly ground black pepper

2 litres/3½ pints chicken stock

300 g/10 oz instant polenta

150 g/5 oz grated fresh parmesan

150 g/5 oz ripe gorgonzola, diced

1 teaspoon fresh thyme leaves

In a large saucepan gently cook the leeks in 85 g/3 oz of the butter until they wilt. Add the greens and continue cooking slowly over a low heat until wilted. Season to taste with salt and pepper.

Bring the chicken stock to the boil, lower the heat and reduce to a simmer. Slowly add the polenta, stirring with a whisk until it is completely blended.

Continue cooking and stirring until the polenta has thickened, and then stir in the remaining butter with the grated parmesan, diced gorgonzola, cooked greens and thyme. Check the seasoning and serve immediately with the roast grouse.

# RICOTTA FRUIT CAKE

225 g/8 oz unsalted butter, softened

225 g/8 oz caster sugar

8 egg yolks + 2 egg whites

grated zest of 2 oranges and 3 lemons

juice of 1 orange

juice of 1 lemon

115 g/4 oz roasted hazelnuts, roughly chopped

200 g/7 oz mixed dried fruits, e.g. whole cranberries, whole cherries, whole blueberries and chopped apricots

275 g/9½ oz ricotta cheese

85 g/3 oz plain flour

crème fraîche and frosted rosemary sprigs, to serve

**For the rosemary syrup:**

115 g/4 oz sugar

115 ml/4 fl oz water

2 sprigs of rosemary

Cream the butter and sugar until pale and fluffy. Add the egg yolks, one by one, beating well between each addition. In a separate bowl, fold the fruit zests and juice, nuts and dried fruit into the ricotta. Add the ricotta and fruit mixture to the creamed cake mix and beat together. Sift in the flour and mix well.

Beat the egg whites to soft peaks. Fold in one large spoonful of the egg whites into the ricotta mix. Once this is amalgamated, fold in the remainder carefully, ensuring that you do not lose too much of the air.

Grease a 23 cm/9 in spring-form cake tin sparingly with vegetable oil. Pour in the cake mixture and bake in a preheated oven at 180°C, 350°F, Gas Mark 4 for about 1¼–1½ hours, or until a skewer inserted into the centre of the cake comes out clean.

Make the rosemary syrup. Put the sugar and water in a pan and place over a medium heat. Stir to dissolve the sugar and then cook until reduced to a syrup. Remove from the heat, add the rosemary and leave to infuse.

When the cake is cool, spike it all over with a fork and dribble the rosemary syrup over the top. Serve the cake, cut into thin slices, with some crème fraîche and frosted rosemary sprigs.

ALDO ZILLI

**ALDO ZILLI** is chef patron of Signor Zilli, Zilli Bar and Zilli Fish in Soho. He is one of London's most flamboyant chefs. Great Italian food and Aldo's legendary sense of humour make these restaurants a magnet for the media and entertainment world. In 1996 he was awarded Best Italian Restaurant, followed by the award for Best Media Restaurant and Favourite Showbiz Restaurant in 1998. Aldo has hosted several television series, including 'Perfect Pasta with Aldo', 'Aldo's Italian Job' and 'Aldo and Friends', and appeared on many cookery programmes. He has written several cookery books, is the resident chef for *The Sun* newspaper and recently made his acting debut, appearing in an episode of 'London Bridge'.

ALDO ZILLI

# MENU

## Aldo Zilli

serves 4

### STARTER

Cream of marrow, red lentil, cabbage and sage soup

### MAIN COURSE

Cotolette di vitello ripiene

Rosemary potatoes and parsnips

Garlic spinach

### DESSERT

Panettone alla Strega

# CREAM OF MARROW, RED LENTIL, CABBAGE AND SAGE SOUP

Here is a warming, typically robust Italian soup to start your Christmas meal. It tastes so delicious that you may wish to double the quantities given and reheat it over the Christmas holiday.

500 g/1 lb 2 oz peeled marrow, cubed

1 onion, chopped

1 celery stick, chopped

1 carrot, chopped

2 potatoes, chopped

100 g/3½ oz white cabbage, thinly sliced

4 tablespoons extra virgin olive oil

50 g/2 oz butter

4 sage leaves, stems removed and chopped

1 teaspoon chopped rosemary

100 g/3½ oz red lentils

pinch of salt

1.8 litres/3 pints vegetable stock

40 g/1½ oz maize flour

5 tablespoons milk or single cream

freshly grated nutmeg

2 tablespoons grated parmesan

flat-leaf parsley, to garnish

Put the prepared marrow, onion, celery, carrot, potatoes and white cabbage in a large saucepan, cover them with water and then simmer gently for 15 minutes. Drain well.

Sauté the vegetables in half of the olive oil and half of the butter in a non-stick saucepan. Add the chopped sage and rosemary, red lentils and a pinch of salt and then cook at a very high temperature for 3 minutes. Add some of the vegetable stock, then reduce the heat and simmer gently for 20 minutes, stirring the soup regularly and adding more stock as needed.

Melt the remaining butter in the rest of the olive oil. Add the maize flour and then whisk together. Add the milk or cream and continue whisking for 10 seconds. Leave to cool before stirring into the soup over a low heat. Stir until slightly thickened.

Add the grated nutmeg and then liquidize the soup in a blender or food processor until smooth. If the soup is too thick, add a little more of the hot stock to thin it down. Add the grated parmesan just before serving and serve garnished with flat-leaf parsley.

# COTOLETTE DI VITELLO RIPIENE

4 large potatoes, thickly sliced

4 large parsnips, quartered or sliced

4 thick lean veal chops (pork can be used as an alternative)

4 slices Parma ham

1 small piece smoked mozzarella, sliced or cubed

4 sage leaves

seasoned flour, for sprinkling

4 tablespoons olive oil

25 g/1 oz butter

115 ml/4 fl oz white wine

2 garlic cloves, peeled

2 rosemary sprigs

chopped flat-leaf parsley, to garnish

**For the garlic spinach:**

2 garlic cloves

4 tablespoons olive oil

50 g/2 oz butter

900 g/2 lb fresh spinach, washed and trimmed

chicken or veal stock

salt and pepper

Cook the potatoes and parsnips in a pan of lightly salted boiling water for 5 minutes. Drain well.

Take a veal chop and, with a very sharp, pointed knife, open the side with no bone. Stuff the chop with a slice of Parma ham, one-quarter of the mozzarella and a sage leaf. Secure with wooden cocktail sticks. Stuff the rest of the chops in the same way and then sprinkle them lightly with a little seasoned flour.

Heat the olive oil and butter in a roasting pan and add the stuffed veal chops. Brown them on both sides and then add the potatoes and parsnips, white wine, peeled garlic cloves and rosemary.

Cook in a preheated oven at 200°C, 400°F, Gas Mark 6 for 20 minutes. If the chops are browning too quickly, cover them with foil for the remainder of the cooking time.

Make the garlic spinach. Sauté the garlic in the olive oil and butter. Add the spinach and a little stock and cook until the spinach wilts and turn bright green. Season to taste with salt and pepper.

Serve the veal chops, sprinkled with parsley, with the roast potatoes, parsnips and garlic spinach.

# PANETTONE ALLA STREGA

1 small Panettone, possibly fruity

300 ml/$\frac{1}{2}$ pint double cream or whipping cream

4 tablespoons caster sugar

225 g/8 oz mixed berries, e.g. raspberries, blueberries and blackberries, chopped

5 tablespoons Strega

caster sugar, for dusting

strawberries, to serve

Cut the Panettone into slices and place them on a baking tray. Bake in a moderate preheated oven at 180°C, 350°F, Gas Mark 4 for about 3–5 minutes, or grill lightly on both sides.

Pour the cream into a bowl and whip until firm, adding the caster sugar to sweeten. Add the mixed berries to the cream and stir in gently. Add a little of the Strega.

Heat the remaining Strega and set it alight. Pour the flaming Strega over the Panettone and, when the flames die down, dust with caster sugar. Serve with the berry cream and some fresh strawberries.

# INDEX